Growth

A.A. WINSTON

A.A. Winston

12522679539
russgh@hotmail.com

Table of Contents

a.k.a. Russ Haddad

GROWTH INTRODUCTION

We all go through different stages in life. New experiences – good, bad, indifferent – make us who we are as we age. We start out young and impressionable.

We move toward a more enlightened station in life as we move into young adulthood. We then progress, if we continue to learn, to realizations and impressions shaped through a variety of interactions and relationships – both direct and indirect.

With **Growth**, the reader follows the evolution of a person through phases of his life. From a teenager/young man who lost his father when he was 12 to a middle-aged man with some wear and tear. He didn't fully know how to show his feelings. To this day as an older man, the author still doesn't always know how to show his feelings. But poetry is an outlet, a sort of safety valve.

While the first volume leans on idealism, the next two provide more depth, intellect, and imagination with a bent toward hope. The author wouldn't necessarily call many of them good, but they are raw and unpolished. The level of sophistication from *Immaturity* increases in style and substance in what follows through further *Maturing* and *Continued Maturation*. The seasoning of time provides greater insight and straightforwardness with an inclination toward irritability.

Growth represents phases of a person's life that he hopes others may relate.

IMMATURITY

I sort of tripped into writing poetry. It started when I was a senior in high school and writing for the school newspaper. I wasn't really a reporter, whatever that means at a high school newspaper. Somehow, I became the newspaper poet in response to something I've since forgotten.

Each edition featured a poem by A.A. Winston, which I adopted as my pen name. I revealed my true identity in the last edition before graduation in a poem entitled, "What's in a Name?" Not many noticed before the reveal, not many after. However, it became part of an initial collection of poems I wrote through college.

In the first of this series, the 75 poems in **Immaturity** includes writings of a teenager/young man who lost his father when he was 12. They are reflections through the eyes and mind of an unseasoned person. A person just starting out and having an idealistic viewpoint on life and relationships. I go from naivete and confusion in Immaturity.

Immaturity is the first phase of a person's life that I hope others may relate.

MIND MELT

The destruction I'm going through
No one can understand.
It is in my mind.
Of high hopes and low confidence
Nothing can replace.

A SPIRIT WITHOUT THE SOUL

A.A. Winston

With all the promises
And statements of good fortune,
Where do we stand today?
The same place as yesterday.

We just sit and wait
Putting our lives on hold.
Turning blue from the lack of air.
Hoping for that quick release
And that feeling of exhilaration.

Frustrations and tensions mount,
To an uncalculatable scale.
So helpless and far away.
Only so much can be taken
Then that line will be crossed.

Everything hinges on so little.
The chosen few know the scoop.
They possess lives in their balance
And act as though they are trivial cares.
In the end it is they who win,
As we fall by the side of the road.

A SHORT ONE

When it comes to dust to dust,
Ashes to ashes.
Some will be grateful,
Most will be deceived.

Growth

TOO CHEAP TO KEEP

A.A. Winston

You spend a lot of money
And cry when the bill reaches the ceiling.
You come to me—
Believing I'm ready to give.
I say no way
But you know it's not true.
Once the hand is in the pocket,
There is no way of getting it back.
When the well runs dry
I get ready to hear a ring.
No reason to pick up—
It could only be you.

For you the merchandise is piled high.
For me the sea of debt is overflowing.
You echo the sounds
That I can only hear.
I seldomly see you weep
Or feel my kind of guilt.
I guess I'm just too cheap to keep.

THE FLIGHT OF SPRING

When two hearts
Become one,
That is the time.
The time we all wait for.
When unending time stops
And the picture becomes clear,
That is the time.
The time we all wait for.

When the mind and body are in synch
And nothing can be said but yes,
That is the time.
The time we all wait for.
The flight of Spring.

Growth

HUMBLE GRATITUDE

I feel the need to thank you.
Without you I could not be who I want to be.
Without you I would have to make believe.
I choose to behold
Something I cannot see.
I cling to this feeling of appreciation.
Hoping it isn't another sort of depravation.
Without you I could not rise to the heights.
Fight for the inalienable rights—
The right to hold you.
The right to say thank you.
I feel the humble gratitude
Of our selective solitude.
Thank you for delivering me
Without the help of deceit.

A.A. Winston

SLUMBER

Sleep.

Tired as I am I cannot sleep.

Things on my mind,

Whistling through my brain.

My head aches with thought making me stay awake.

People, places, and situations.

How will I handle them?

What will I say?

Sleep will help clear these thoughts.

But nerves hold me slumberless.

When all is resolved

And I feel comfortable again,

Then there will be time

To sleep.

Growth

THE UNKNOWING NIGHT

A.A. Winston

Icicles melt from the heat of the sun.

The desire dwindles from the lack of activity.

Moods shift swiftly

Like a weighted pendulum.

Day turns to night.

The pace slows as well as the heartbeat.

The night is cold,

As cold as some stares.

The icicles begin to re-form.

They hang so low.

Nothing can stop their growth

Except the warmth of the morning sun.

But there are no guarantees

Just broken promises.

All we can do is hope for the sun.

And we must wait through the long night.

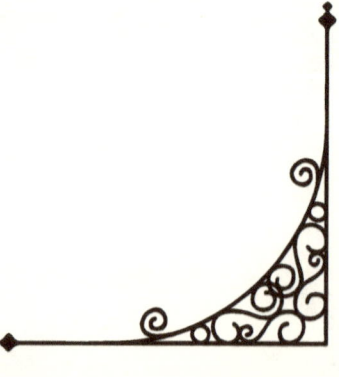

GETTING IT STRAIGHT

Why do I let the world spin me?
I'm on a ride that won't slow down.
The almighty dollar has me running,
Unable to catch what breath I may have left.

I need the paper bag
For my head feels like a balloon.
Floating in a zone
Unlike anyone has seen before.

The ones around me seem to be big time,
If they would let go of the small time.
Until then the tug continues.

Whose priorities hold precedence?
Can't be theirs.
I don't know who they are
Or understand what they are.

Let them live their lives
And leave me to mine.
My actions make little sense.
But are uniquely designed to set me apart.

Growth

THE MIX

A.A. Winston

You scream,
Like a tiger roars
But still, you stick your head in the sand
As quick as an ostrich.
Sight unseen
Like the camouflaged chameleon.
You swing from problem to problem,
Like a monkey swing from limb to limb.
On the outside you're a peacock
But on the inside a rhino.
Venting frustrations like a bull,
While purring like a cat.
You can act as refined as a thoroughbred
But choose to act as dirty as a rat.
In this world of animal kingdoms
No wonder the human is so small,
It can't be one without the many.

CREATIVITY

It's quite the baffling thing.
When the process begins
It is hard to stop.
It can hit at any time
And last only briefly.
Sometimes it seems to last an eternity.
Its course cannot be charted
Or even plotted.
You can't control its impact,
But have a big influence.
It can give an exhilarating feeling
When it hits the right chord.
It packs power and sensitivity.
It chooses the pattern.
It tends to get the message across no matter the style.
Never wonder where it comes from
It can't be explained.
It just perplexes.
Just let it flow
And run its course.
Because all too soon you'll wonder where it went.
Creativity doesn't only happen between 9 and 5.

HUH?

A.A. Winston

Ever think something was that way,
Only for it to turn out to be this way?
Ever find your head spinning,
While others remained steady?
Ever ask a good question,
And never get the desired answer?
Ever solve a problem in a logical manner,
Only to find the response a dumbfounded look?
Ever try to see through another's eyes,
Finding the view blocked by some sort of cloud?
Ever get the feeling no one is listening,
When all they say is—
Huh?

REQUIEM FOR THE DEAD

We have forgotten our dead.
The ones we love.
Our lives are much too lively.
It is so typical to say we miss them
Only to turn our backs on them.
It makes me wonder how it will be
When I sing my swan song.

The processions will be long.
The tears shed will be many.
But when I'm finally put to rest,
The memory of me
Will always be
That I lived for the ones I loved.
Then I can live with being forgotten.

Growth

RETROSPECTION

I miss my days of yesterday.
Through my youth I have become elderly.
I've seen too much to just turn my head.
I've heard the word of many misgivings
Only to realize the true realities.

A.A. Winston

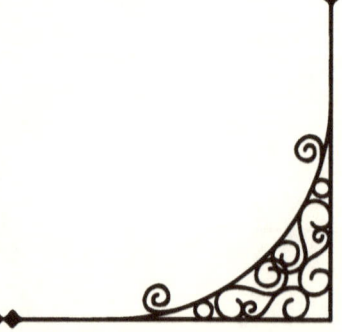

IT'S BEEN SAID

It's been said before
That I don't care anymore.
But it's not true
And you know, too.
If you give up now
It's gone for good.
Don't let it happen
For you'll be as sorry
As I will be.

It's also been said I don't care
For anyone except myself,
But for you this is not true.
You are the one I need
You are the one I care for.
So don't close the door
Just as I walk in.
Let me be yours and
Let it be said...
That you are mine.

Growth

THE SECRET CLUE

A.A. Winston

Penniless and poor.

What are we looking for?

The light at the end?

The pot of gold?

Accept it as it is.

These are too unreachable.

One can't take a giant step

Before the little ones are forged.

Look, listen.

This is the clue.

This is the secret.

SECRETS OF THE UNTELLING

Secrets untold.

Quite unheard of.

Silence crowds the room.

Making its presence known.

Whispers screaming in the air,

Filling everyone's ears.

Things not known

Benefit some but may hurt many others.

Foolish rumors may be sprung

As if the boy took his thumb out of the dike.

Conflicting stories run rampant,

With no control

And less believability.

Then one steps for

Revealing to others

What they should not know.

Growth

REVEALING DARKNESS

A.A. Winston

Falling into a deep, dark hole.

Inescapable, unending.

No way out,

Just keep tumbling.

The darkness is scary

But somehow adventurous.

It may seem like punishment

But in a way it's advantageous.

No perception.

No deception.

Unlike the light.

THE WRITTEN WORD

Crumbling and tossing

The ideas seemed complete.

The end becomes the beginning.

One line can screw you up

And make the rest sound sad.

Yet you plug away until it's right.

Still, it may be bad.

Frustration sets in

And cuts off the flow.

Time away from paper

Helps make the pen work wonders.

Growth

When the product is finished

And the words are read,

Pride should be felt.

The criticisms welcomed.

The appreciation of the written word valued.

HIGH AND INSIDE

A.A. Winston

Sitting pretty,
On your pedestal.
Looking down
Seeing those looking up.
High up.
Low down.
Where's the in between?
The level is predestined.
But kept undercover.
Brought out by confidence,
Determination and security.
Extend your heights
And expectations.
Then stand proud,
On your pedestal.

IS ANYBODY OUT THERE?

When I turn around
And look through the door I see a mist
Clouding my view.

No matter where I turn
It's always the same,
Things being twisted,
Spun around in circles.
Is anybody out there?
Waiting for that lonely dream.
Hoping tonight's the night.

Is anybody around?
Someone to talk to,
Wanting to take hold of.

You can't keep running
Just face the facts
It ain't so bad
And it has to get better.

Growth

I didn't say it was easy,
Never would have.
It's your confusions
That need to be worked out.
Is anybody out there?
Waiting for that lonely dream
Hoping tonight's the night.

Is anybody around?
Someone to talk to,
Wanting to take hold of.
Doubts and recollections
Leave me in a suspended state.
Lack of control
Pushes me over the edge.
Things happen too quickly.
The pace is hasty.
The world is turbulent and unforgiving.
I have to wonder.

Is anybody out there?
Waiting for that lonely dream.
Hoping tonight's the night.

Is anybody around?
Someone to talk to, wanting to take hold of.

A.A. Winston

THE LESSON

I want to ask the questions
That no one will answer.
I want to command the orders
That no one follows.
I want to teach
What no one wants to learn.
I want to say so many words
That no one can piece together.
I want to speak a special language
Never heard by anyone.
I need to learn so many things
The things no one will ever teach.

Growth

PLAY DEEP

Go back, back, back.

To when you were against the fence.

A question arose,

Do I have a chance?

People told you only one way to find out.

That way is to go for it.

Don't give up

Or you'll regret.

If you have the promise

And the skill,

Don't run away

Go straight ahead.

When against the fence again,

Decisions will be made.

For good, for bad

But they are something you can't turn back.

PASSING ON

Another loss.

They keep going down

One by one.

It's not just the men

But the women and children, too.

Injustice can't stop the crimes.

The blood will run.

Even after the river's dry.

Growth

PRECIOUS FRIENDS

A.A. Winston

Don't smoke?
Don't drink?
What are you a freak?
This is what they say.
This is how they react.

Looked down upon
And not accepted.
The pressure of friends, The pressure of family.
Whom do you choose?
Precious friends, of course.
For they care for you
Less than you know!

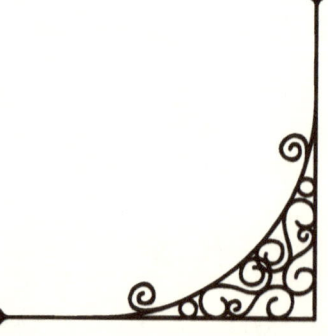

THE FINALS

Time travels so fast.
Our trek started four long years ago.
Now it has come down to this.
Many things have passed on by.
Many things have changed.
We've seen the good
And lots of the bad.
We've all prevailed
And made the most of the least,
Rediscovering something which was lost.
Pride and devotion and dedication
Brought back from the depths.
The thing which spurs the weak and strong alike.
The thing which will carry most
To the heights of success
With each and every endeavor.

Growth

NO FOUNDATION, NO ANCHOR

A.A. Winston

Nothing in this world is attached.

Everything moves in an up and down motion.

Detachment causes so much chaos.

People float with no direction,

Aimlessly seeking fortune and fame,

Hunting down that American dream.

Attitudes change like New England weather.

There is no constant.

The ebb and flow are everlasting.

Mixed up emotions lead our lives.

Knowing what you want helps,

Knowing what you need is no handicap,

Though it is all too uncommon.

Existence in society is petty and perverse.

Society dwells with no foundation and no anchor.

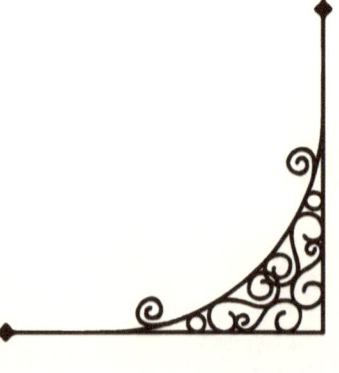

THE FEELING

My world is tumbling.

Maybe even crumbling.

What I have worked so hard to get

Keeps eluding me.

The satisfaction of someone saying yes.

The idea of being the best.

I can always see it coming

But I never want to look.

The writing on the wall is so profound,

But all I read are meaningless words.

Growth

FOR AN INSTANCE

I didn't see you coming
In the rear-view mirror.
Like a flashback
You popped into my mind.
Like a shadow
It was never everlasting.

A.A. Winston

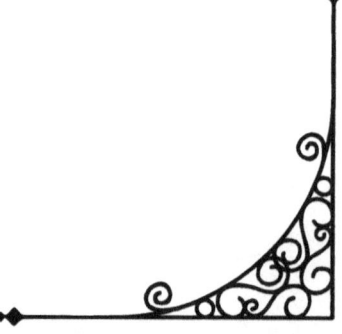

LONESOME DESIRE

It's time to go home
But you're all alone
Seeking the company of someone's despair.
When the anger builds
The hunger fades away.

MISUNDERSTANDABLE

You always say a lot of something
But it sounds like a lot of nothing.

Your words are the same
But differ in meaning.
A bunch of phrases
In a mixed menagerie.

A.A. Winston

EVERY INCH OF THE WAY

Looking in your window
Seeing nothing but darkness.
Not knowing what to do
I sit and wait for you.
Your stubborn insensitivity
Is hard to contend with
But something I can deal with
And something I can break down.
You think you're right
But I keep you in sight
Every inch of the way
Until we are together.

I send roses to your office
And cards to your house
Though it seems to me
You're just blowing me off.

Running around in circles
Waiting for a reaction
You just ignore me
As if no response was my goal.

Growth

You think you're right
But I keep you in sight
Every inch of the way
Until we are together.

Suddenly you turn around
And take me by surprise
Noticing all my activities
And showing that you care.

When I finally catch up with you
There is just one thing to do
Hop on for the ride
And hang on tight.
You thought you were right
As I kept you in sight
Every inch of the way
After we are together.

A.A. Winston

SYMPTOMS

You can feel it coming on.

Coming on strong.

The chills, the shrills, the thrills.

These are the symptoms.

Of devotion,

Of insecurity,

Of love.

Looking around to see who's looking.

Trying to catch the eye of someone.

Someone that just isn't there.

These are the symptoms.

Dressing to impress.

Trying to make someone notice.

The eyes of the world are all upon you.

But the eyes you want are not around.

These are the symptoms.

Of devotion,

Of insecurity,

Of love.

Growth

_____

Going out to lunch.
wanting to be part of someone's life.
Having to be with someone.
Seeing that someone gratifies you.
These are the symptoms.

Of devotion,
Of insecurity,
Of love.

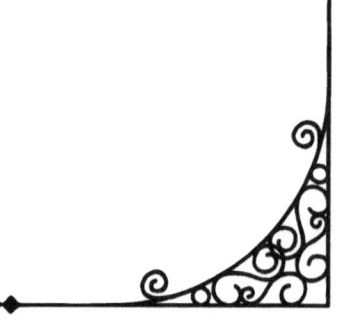

CARRIE ANN

I look into your eyes,
What do I see?
I see confusion and pain.
Some caused by me.
Some caused by you.
That is why I can't walk away
From Carrie Ann.

When I'm in your company,
If feels too right.
When I'm alone,
I wish you were here.
When I see that reassuring smile
I find it hard to walk away
From Carrie Ann.

Sometimes you make me mad,
Other times you make me glad.
Many times, you make me so sad.
Making you cry was not my plan,
Watching those tears fall from your face
Makes it hard for me to walk away
From Carrie Ann.

Growth

We've made decisions, we've made mistakes,
We've got everything,
Everything to make it work.
But for us to work,
I must walk away
From Carrie Ann.

A.A. Winston

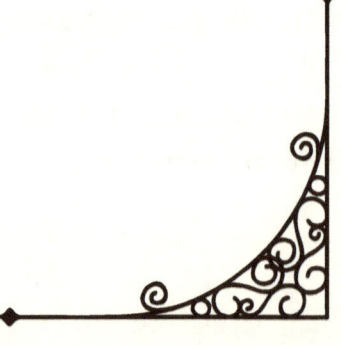

MODERN SOCIETY

Modern people
Can't relate to modern problems
Because they're living
In those big modern homes.
Society dwells in this way,
Nowadays.
The ones who care can't afford it.
The ones who can don't care.
Changes come,
Changes go.
Just like the seasons.
The Spring has the ideas
But the Fall won't listen.
And in the end
Nothing changes.

Growth

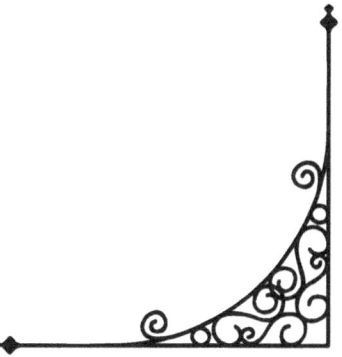

PAST, PRESENT, FUTURE

The road is long.
It has many twists and turns.
The next thing you know you hit a dead end.
But all dead ends can be opened.
If you hit one, don't look back,
The past is done and over,
Stay put in the present
And think of where you're going.
Then head for the future with new ideas.
You are the only one,
Who knows what is right for you?
The influence of others just confuses.
Listen to yourself.
Be happy with yourself.
No regrets should be taken.
You are the past, present and future.

A.A. Winston

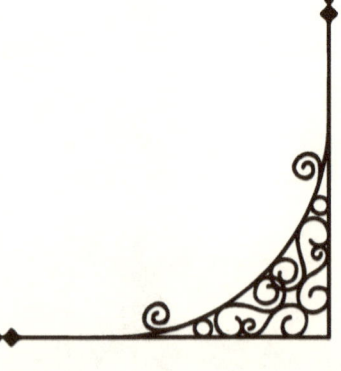

DREAMS

Dreams,

From your own reality.

Flirting with time.

Deciding what's right.

Through the scope of life.

Mine, yours, all of ours.

It's like an hourglass.

Don't let it slip away.

And never give up what's important.

Never give up your

Dreams.

Growth

CONTEMPLATIONS

What's wrong with life?
Some people are satisfied.
Most are not.
What does it take?
What do they like?
They say people who have less
Appreciate more.
How can that be?
It may be true,
But who's to say?
Not I, nor you,
But life's experiences
Will show the way.

A.A. Winston

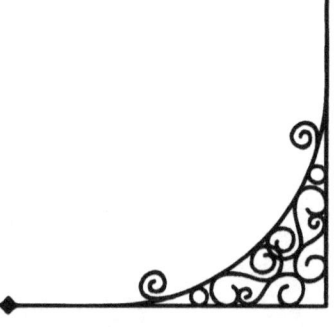

REALIZATIONS

It's everywhere,

You can see it,

You can sense it,

But you cannot always express it.

It's a mystery,

And it can hit you at any moment.

It's disguised,

Hidden behind closed doors,

If it cannot be stated in words,

Then your face and actions

Will say it.

It feels strange to feel it,

But don't deny it.

Once you realize it's for real,

It will take care of itself.

Don't be afraid,

You're not alone,

Love is universal.

Growth

WHAT'S IT ALL ABOUT?

You see things once,
You see things twice,
But you never see what it's all about.
You're mesmerized by complacency
You have to learn to appreciate things.
Take them in stride
One day at a time.
Don't get caught looking over your shoulder
The next thing you know there's someone behind you.
Keep your sights set on the future.
Just remember, life is short,
You have to live your every moment,
Live it to the fullest.
Just have fun
And be happy.
That's what it's all about.

A.A. Winston

MOMENTS

While sitting in the recliner
Watching the football game—my mind drifts...
I start to think back,
To when I was younger,
When I had to worry less of things.
It was easier then.
I remember my father,
Laying on the couch,
And me propped against his belly,
Watching sports on TV,
We enjoyed that together,
I enjoyed that time with him.
Those are the special memories I have of my father.
He, along with my mother, was always there,
That is why I love them both,
And always will.

Growth

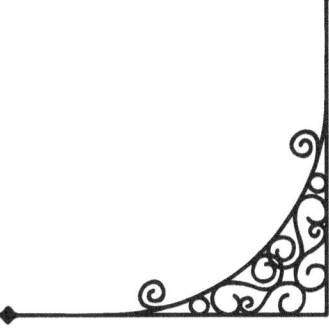

THE FINE LINE

Back and forth we go.
How do you know which way we will turn?
Could we be balanced and remain in the center?
We can try our best to keep things peaceful,
But trying too hard can break it all down.

You say I will pull you to the left.
I say you will push me to the right.
We won't know until it happens.
Only soothsayers predict the future.

A.A. Winston

Let's stick to basics,
Stay close to the edge,
So, we can catch ourselves if we fall.
A danger we should be aware of.

The center is so hard to maintain
Each expects so much of one another
And coping with the pressure
Causes a straying of the parties.

Keep it simple is complex
But a goal we should set.
For it to last
We must not overcrowd our limited space.

Let's give it a whirl
And see where we land.
If we want it to, we can make it.

Growth

INNER QUALITY

A.A. Winston

An Inner Quality.
Owned by one,
Owned by many.
It should not be taken for granted.
We so often expect so much
Because we are not satisfied with ourselves.
The first impression
Means too much.
We give up before
That Inner Quality is discovered.

The Inner Quality is hard to find in some.
We have to dig deep under the surface.
And in cases
The search is worthless.
But the pursuit is always there.

We must remember no one is alike.
So that Inner Quality can be masqueraded.
There is no time for petty hatred.
Taking people for what they are worth
And not placing a price on them,
Their Inner Qualities will arise.

THE SPECTRUM

On top, on the bottom,
Somewhere in between.
Which do you prefer?
Which is better?
Why have either,
When you can have it all.
Success is stability.
Combining top and bottom
Gives you the middle.
The place with the mix
And the right balance.
The place in the Spectrum
Which is least populated
And least desired.

Growth

DISCONTENT

Yes, today I am in Discontent.

I ask myself, "why?"

I reply, "because I have taken wrong turns."

Somehow, some way I must get untracked.

Little by little

I will lose my Discontent,

For I plan to change my attack.

There is only one way to go

And that is up.

The day is coming

When I shall be content.

Then things will be

The way they should be.

For me, for you, for everyone.

But today I am in Discontent.

A.A. Winston

FRIENDSHIP VERSUS SOMETHING MORE

We say love,

Do we mean it?

Is it just good friendship?

Or something unexplainable?

We have a habit

Of cutting it short

Even though neither wants to.

What is the problem?

What do we mean?

Time together,

Time apart,

This is how we'll know it's right.

If this is survivable,

Then we are survivable.

Growth

THE LIMIT

A.A. Winston

The Limit—
The point where success or failure is unstoppable.
It is the maximum point of pushing yourself,
No matter the circumstances.

The Limit—
Enables you to conquer any obstacle.
There is no choice at this point.
Forward is your only direction.
And has to be followed through.

The Limit—
Can be a foe as well as friend.
Pushing too far causes friction.
The breakdown is thorough
And may not always be controllable.
Pressure hits all at once.

The Limit—
Makes you do what's not expected.
It keeps you going When you're down.
It can earn the respect,
But not always the honor.
That is what is called—
The Limit.

ALL AVAILABLE OPTIONS

Looking at your beat-up junk,
Comparing it to your beat-up life.
A decision is made to go for something better.
A new wheel to sit behind,
A new path of life to lead.

Tracking down that new car,
There are lots of things to consider.
Life is like that new car,
You look at all available options.

Growth

At first you think, "stick to the basics;"
Then your mind wanders and yearns for more.
A fire engine red sports car,
That's what you want.
Nothing simple, nothing plain.

But looks aren't everything.
Tilt wheel, electric seats, power windows.
To top it off AM/FM stereo cassette.
Personality is guaranteed.

Tracking down that new car,
There are lots of things to consider.
Life is like that new car,
You look at all available options.

Dead ends appear wherever you turn.
The salesmen lead you astray.
Saying one thing, doing another.
Lost in the shuffle
Ready to give up.

Then before you know it,
Out comes from nowhere,
What you didn't expect to find.
It's right in front of your eyes.

Upon reviewing your available options,
You think back again.
Life is like buying this new car.
Something good can come from bad.
You must look at all the available options.

A.A. Winston

CONCENTRATION

It is a facet that enables success.

If you don't have it,

You'll keep wandering.

Concentration is your goal,

It is your purpose.

Without it life has no meaning.

Distractions on the outside

Make it hard to concentrate

But if you want it bad enough

It will persevere.

Growth

THE END

A.A. Winston

It takes time for me,
Takes time for you.
It was long
And sometimes bitter.
If we had better communication,
We could have lasted a lifetime.
But it's over now,
Nothing can stop it,
We can't go back,
This is the end.

Decisions were to be made.
By me, by you.
And we made the ones
We thought were right.
They were in our best interest,
and there's no backing down.

'Cause it's over now,
Nothing can stop it,
We can't go back,
This is the end.

Starting over with new people
Can be so hard.
But is something that has to be done.
We have to accept
Our new endeavors,
We are embarking
On a new beginning.
Seeing each other with other people
Will hurt for a while.
But the hurting stops,
and it becomes easier.
Pain and hurt
are the things that make experiences.
For now, let's hold on to our memories
And go on.

'Cause it's over now,
Nothing can stop it,
We can't go back,
This is the end.

Growth

IT'S OVER

When you told me I thought it untrue.
You said goodbye with no reason at hand.
I tried to understand but couldn't,
As you said it's over.

We agreed to be friends.
I didn't think it would work.
It's been up and down,
Ever since you said it's over.

That day I thought I had a chance.
You were kind and receptive.
But when I went to your house later
You ignored me once again.
I still don't know what the problem was
Or why you had to say it's over.

A.A. Winston

FAMILY TRAIT

In the struggle to get ahead
We always seem to stumble and fall.
No matter how hard we may try
Our faces seem flatter than most.
That is what's known as the family trait.

A THOUGHT

A.A. Winston

Thinking is quite unconscious
One never knows when it will begin
Or when it will end.
Some may say it is unceasing.
There is no art to thinking
Nature takes its course in its capacity.
Problems are solved,
Inner turmoil diminished.
Too much thinking can cause bad.
But so often it makes one feel good.
This is contrary to this world,
For it does so little
Thinking.

ATTITUDES

I don't care what you do.

I don't care what you say.

I just care about me and mine.

That's what counts.

That's what I believe.

THE MIND

Just scream and shout
Don't forget what it's all about.
Seen the good, seen the bad,
Seen it all twice again.
What you get out Is what you put in.
No second guessing
When it's on the line.
Up, down, in the middle.
Don't forget what it's all about
Just scream and shout.

A.A. Winston

DETERMINATION

Determination gets you things.
Whether they're good or bad
It's up to you.
But determination is the only way
To get what you want.
Ignoring this as a need
For getting ahead
Can injure projections of a future.

Determination is the never-ending want
And the never losing sight of achievement,
It is said to be grim.
Hard work usually is.
But this should not stop one
From setting goals placed upon himself.

Determination doesn't always make you happy,
But it keeps the door open for happiness
When the mission is complete.
It enables you to take that next step.

Determination plays games.
Games that make you win.

Growth

TREND REVERSAL

A.A. Winston

Lessons unlearned
Lead to problems.
Gone unnoticed
Makes it worse.
After a period
There's no turning back.
This is the pleasure of being human.
Once a mistake is made
It can be corrected.
The solutions are always there
But not always easily accessible.
No mountain is unconquerable,
It's just hard finding those willing to climb.

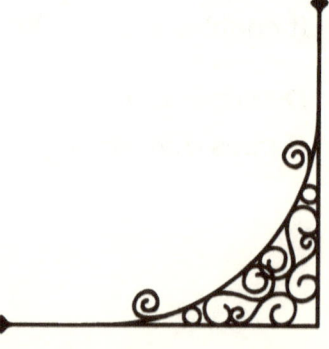

A SPECIAL REWARD

Writing down your thoughts offers a certain reward.

They can be shaped into so many things.

Surprises soon follow

When a good line appears.

Pride and joy surface

For they always come from the heart.

ANSWERS TO QUESTIONS

I have no answers to tell you.

I was hoping you had some for me.

My confusion is long sustained

And yours is quite evident, too.

Ask the questions

Then walk away.

I'm just a recording.

My opinions are formed by what I've heard.

So, if you are seeking a voice of reason,

Look within yourself

Before relying of someone else's tastes.

A.A. Winston

SERVICE HELP

May I have some service, please.
I have some major needs.

You may be my kind of help.
If not, then so be it.
There is no satisfaction in being unsatisfied.

I will have to move on
If you prefer to mind your own business.
Who needs you anyway?

A shortage of good help is conspicuous.

Growth

THE AWAITING

Waiting for your voice to call
Is like waiting for the snow to fall.
A constant game
With a prize of constant heartache.
The perfect time is still a long time away.
Dealing with you is like dealing with a doctor,
Always waiting to hear if I'm going to live or die.
The day is coming
And I will be waiting
For you to come serenading.

A.A. Winston

REACH OUT

It's been a long time
But it is the right time.
When I feel the need to reach out for a love
I reach for you to find someone to hold.

WHERE'S THE RELATIONSHIP?

A.A. Winston

Where do we go from here?
Will this relationship evolve
Or just revolve?
Maybe dissolve is the right pronunciation.
You got into it
Now get me out of it.
You have your way,
We're taking it slow.
Something says this is too comfortable.
For one of us at least.
Let me ask,
Is this your idea of a relationship?

CORNUCOPIA

Peering at my cornucopia,

I think of giving thanks,

Not only for the food I have.

But for my family and friends.

It is that time of year

When all have such an opportunity.

The closeness of generations

Sharing in one moment.

Growth

MELODY MEDLEY I

At first, I thought it easy.
I thought it was based on "Honesty."
And simply "A Matter of Trust."
"I Don't Want to Be Alone Anymore."
So, I'm going to "Tell Her About It."
One of my "Seven Wishes" would be
That you stay "Just the Way You Are."
For me "The Search Is Over."
"Everybody Has a Dream"
And mine seems like a "Fantasy."
But "She's Got a Way"
When she takes my hand
To "Take Me Home."
When I look back
I will have to admit "I've Loved These Days."
And I will be "Keeping the Faith"
That "Someday" we will meet and say, "Hello Again."

MELODY MEDLEY II

The "Falling of The Rain"
Reminded me of "Laura."
She always wanted the "Easy Money"
And I was one of "The Last of the Big Time Spenders."
She was the "Big Shot"
Who took control of "My Life."
I was just an "Innocent Man."
She started as a "Smalltown Girl."
"Looking for Love."
But then her "True Colors" began to shine.
Receiving everything she wanted.
A fortress around her heart.
With "All the Love" I tried to give
She persisted to be good only to herself.
I once asked, "How Much Did You Get for Your Soul?"
And she replied, "Only the Good Die Young,"
As if she were "Sleeping with the Television On."
It didn't take me long to realize
Why everybody loves her now.

Growth

MELODY MEDLEY III

The "Voices of America's Sons"
Are screaming down "Mercy Street."
They are the "Victims"
Of "All You Zombies."
The public asks, "Where Do the Children Go?"

Let's "Celebrate Youth"
And save them from being "Swallowed by the Cracks."
Let them go out and find their own glory
Before it's too late,
When we cannot hear the orchestra
But only the sound of "Goodbye."

A.A. Winston

MELODY MEDLEY IV

Upon the "Wedding Day"
And entering "The Church of the Poison Mind"
You're "Between A Laugh and A Tear."

One must wonder "What Does It Take?"
For nobody stays together anymore.
They say "No One Is to Blame."
But as "Day by Day" goes by
You wonder why.

At the "Start of the Breakdown"
As you're thinking of "Throwing It All Away,"
You step into the other shoes,
Look through the "Lost and Found,"
Stop the shouting and start the listening.

"All the Voices"
"Melting In the Sun"
Have you "Hanging on A Heartbeat."
When it seems you are "'Missing Persons'
'Worlds Apart,'"
Remember "It's Only Love"
"And that's all."

SHOCKED

And if I said to you to beware,
You turn to me and say I have no fear.
I return with a look of despair,
Relating everything to an electric chair.

A.A. Winston

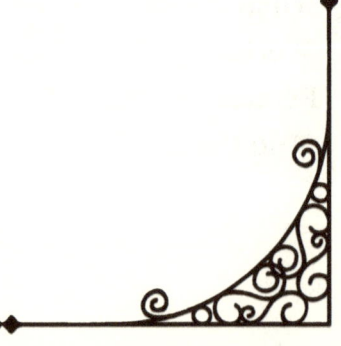

SHOW AND TELL

Put your feet back on the ground.

Nothing but nosebleeds up there anyway.

Stick to what you know,

Place your talent on display.

Create and promote your own show.

Let the dreams fall into reality.

Growth

WHO IS TO BLAME?

I never said that I was sorry
And I probably never will.
It's a shame we came to this.
The loss of language led to worry.
And soon thereafter a departure.
The blame rests on our shoulders.

A.A. Winston

HOW DO YOU GET THERE?

The staircase is broken.

No way to get to heaven.

Try a step ladder...

Not sturdy enough.

Maybe a rope will pull me up...

Too bad it's not long enough.

What shall I use instead?

Call a general contractor to repair them.

Do it yourself—

Money and soul may be saved.

Growth

ON AND ON ...

On and on we go along.

Unpressured by time.

Uncluttered by space.

Open is the path of life.

The sin of ignorance

Lays at death's door,

Still alive and allowed to thrive.

Inspired by our own desires.

Open eyes with closed minds.

A.A. Winston

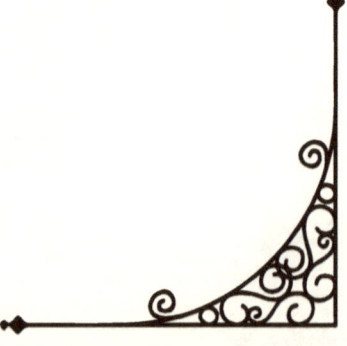

DAZED

Of the lost words I did not speak.

I don't think they can be recovered.

At least not in the same vain

Or in the same context.

What I meant to say got lost in my head.

Lost in the chasm known as my brain.

Unable to reflect on their substance and worth.

Growth

THE WAY I SEE IT

The way I see it
We were meant to be.
Maybe I'm a romantic
But that's just the way it seems to me.
You question my strength
While I have always prevailed.
Maybe you're just looking for an excuse.
That's the way I see it.
The way I see it
Your concerns are valid.
Maybe times will be tough
But we'll never know at the rate we go.
I know we've never been a couple.
A pair of shoes never in the same closet.
Maybe you believe the truth will hurt too much.
That's just the way I see it.

A.A. Winston

MATURING

We all go through different stages in life. New experiences – good, bad, indifferent – make us who we are as we age.

We start out young and impressionable. We move toward a more enlightened station in life as we move into young adulthood.

In the second book of this series, the 75 poems **in** *Maturing* includes writings of a college graduate embarking on a professional life taking on more complex situations and relationships. They are reflections of someone full of vim and vinegar and a greater sense of awareness. Yet, they hold the line on idealism and naivete.

Maturing is the second phase of a person's life that I hope others may relate.

Growth

PINNING THE TAIL

It was late in November
And all I could see was my future slipping away.
The story from the South Pacific
Your being stranded on an island
Reflecting on your meaning of truth.

The cold of winter still hangs on
Yet the truth still eludes.
Your words of discouragement
Lead me to decide.
I sit here lonely
Waiting to make up my mind.

Running circles
Ending at square one.
It's too hard to search for answers
When the answers are right there.
With my eyes closed.
Spun three times around.
My finger always lands on you.

A.A. Winston

I KNOW THE REACTION

If I ever told you
It's time to move on.
Go our separate ways.
How would you react?

If I told you, would it make me happier?
Not to get away from you
But to simply lead another life.

Avoidance of what lies ahead.
Avoidance of what is already dead.
Not saying what I must know
Because I don't know how you'd react.

Plans were made
But wrongly agreed to.
Something said sooner, better
But I was afraid of how you'd react.

It's not an easything.
The timing never is.
I screwed up
Nothing left to say.

Disappointing many expectations
Can't help that.
I must do what's right for me.
In the long run for us.

No matter your reaction
The storyline played itself out.
No new chapters to add.
Hard to figure we both don't see it.

There is no good way to dish out hurt
For the hurt goes both ways.
I hate to do this from the blind side
Because I know what your reaction will be.

A.A. Winston

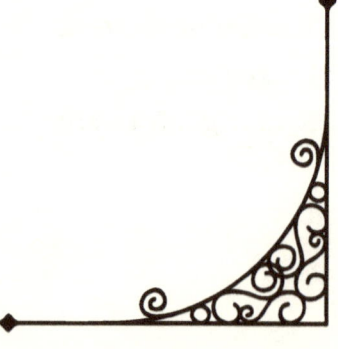

RED

Time to get naked.

No time to get peaked.

You look a little flushed

Don't let the moment go down the toilet.

The Tidy Bowl Man can't help you now.

Time to look to Trojan Man

For your protection

And your sanctuary.

It's too late to walk away

The matter is at hand.

Face your need.

Take as much as you want.

Growth

WHO DO YOU WANT?

Being with someone
And you at the same time.
Kissing the one I'm with
And kissing you, too.
Mirror images
In a two-way mirror.
One seen
The same unaware.

A.A. Winston

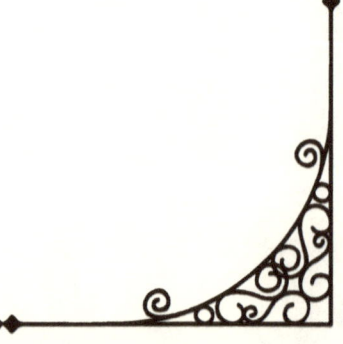

LOST IN THE PAGES

Remember me?

I'm the one in L.A.

Who thinks he's not worth anything.

I guess I've been proven right.

Relief to Florida.

Relief to Hawaii.

Immediate responses.

No relief for me.

First, you take the word of four white men.

We rebel, still seen as negative.

Politicians appear for photo ops.

No one has heard from them since.

I still wait for the songs of benefit,

For the money to rebuild

Yet I still sit in the dirt.

The ashes.

The waste.

Growth

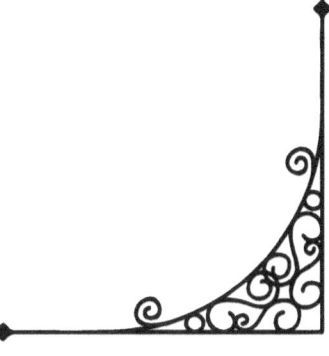

ROMANTICALLY INVOLVED

Slow dancing
In the twi-night.
Stars shining Moon aglow.
Holding you close
Hand in hand.
Your head on my shoulder
My cheek in your soft hair.
Fragile is the moment
Of me and you as we.
Whispers in your ear
Noted as sweet nothings
But knowing it's much more.

A.A. Winston

NEMESIS

I don't want to talk about you.

I don't want to think of you.

It always leads to my demise.

Broken hinges on a door,

What do you surmise?

Tasteless words on my tongue.

Wasted space in my brain.

The closed sign is hanging in the window

So, you can't come back into my life.

Growth

THE HEAT

She was the tempest.
I was the teapot.
She was in my blood,
Turning on the pressure
Bringing me to a boil.

A.A. Winston

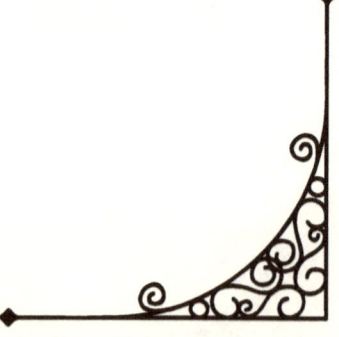

SHOULD I DARE?

It's not up to me.
It's not up to you.
Who is it up to anyway?

Pass it on to someone else.
Leave me alone.
Give me a break
From all this awareness.

I don't need a heart on a sleeve
Just a reality to believe.
Hand it to me, but—
Please don't make me do my share.
I would hate for people to know
That underneath I care.

Growth

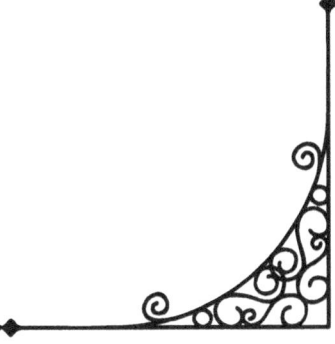

LULLA-BYE

Hysteria in the eyes.

Melodrama from afar.

These are the children.

The fortunes of our future.

Sing them the lullabies.

May they sleep tight tonight.

A.A. Winston

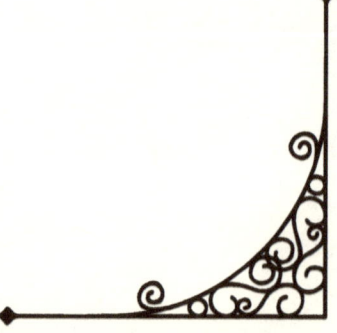

A DIFFERENT PERSPECTIVE

Give me one thing.

Give me two.

Give me something else to dream of.

Something besides you.

What more can I say?

What more can I do?

Self-explanation

For another point of view.

Growth

OPEN BOOK

Have you heard the end of the story?

It's not quite over yet.

There are still some chapters left.

Or is it just a re-write?

A.A. Winston

MEDIACRACY

Satellites link us up.

Television tunes us out.

Radio keeps playing the same old songs.

Drugs can leave us incomplete.

Think of mediacracy.

Think of the hypocrisy.

Growth

FALLEN FRIENDSHIP

A.A. Winston

You said you would be there,
But when I turned around
You seemed to disappear.
Your love was to be forever,
But when I called on that love
I never got an answer.
You said I could talk to you,
But when I said hello
You seemed aloof.
You told me you would always help,
But when I needed help
You suggested someone else.
Now who can I turn to,
The wall has better ears.

PERIODICAL PUPILS

I've come full circle

Around this straight line.

Long routes taken for short trips.

Why didn't someone tell me

This was how it was going to be.

Too many lessons

Being taught by the wrong teachers.

The equation of life

Complicated by "1+1" and "See Spot run."

Growth

LISTEN

Listen to the music
For what it might say.
Listen to the music
For it will not lead you astray.

A.A. Winston

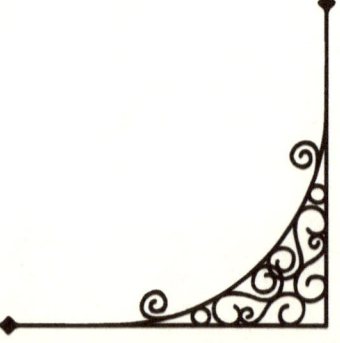

A SIMPLE VALENTINE

I didn't buy a card
Or just some heart.
I hope you know how I feel
For then you'd know it was for real.
I speak it in my mind
And this is the best time to speak it aloud,
I say it very rarely,
But there's no denying
That I love you dearly.

Growth

JUST FRIENDS, OKAY?

After all, I'd hate to complicate things.
I know our time is well spent now,
So why change things.
I'm comfortable with our present situation.
Aren't you?

Yes, you're right.
No need to fix what's not broke.
But I'm tired of your opposite actions.
If you say it, live by it.
I agree to your plea,
And won't cross the line,
As long as you see fit
To save me from the fall.
Okay, friend!

So, it's a pact.
The stress is alleviated.
The feelings spared.
The hurt hidden.
But the complication remains.

A.A. Winston

FORGET IT NOT

We all manifest our destiny.
Each endeavor leads to the next.
Whenever we feel some security
We must be aware of disparity.
In all our mutual understanding
We tend to forget civility.

Growth

YEA OR NAY

I want to know
Today and now
Which way it will go
Yes or no.
Push me away
Or pull me through.
Tell me what you want to say.

A.A. Winston

PAINFUL PRICE

You can inflict the pain

But remember blood leaves a stain.

You can keep the vice

But remember,

You have to pay the price.

Growth

ISOLATION

I need the touch of a miracle's hand
To a capacity from which I cannot understand.
So many worlds still left uncreated
To all man's desires desecrated.
Interests in mind pinpointed in time
Aggregated by the anointed crime.

A.A. Winston

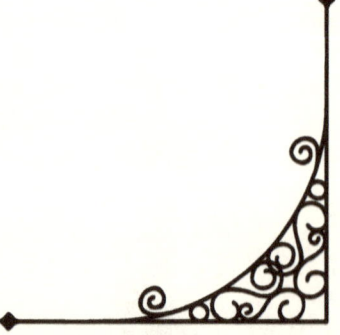

OUT OF REACH

I hold out my hands
To hold onto something.
But all I grasp
Are the grains of sand
Sifting through my fingers.
Powerless to all of beings
I clench my fist
To keep hold of the rose.
Time cannot contain these sorry ideals.

Growth

CAUSAL RELATION

When the glass breaks
It's the pane that hurts.
Just like everything else,
The effect is the result
Of the cause.

A.A. Winston

EXPLANATION, PLEASE

You don't want the truth.

You just want someone who tells you

What you want to hear.

I know that's not what you say

But you make that perfectly clear.

I don't know what it is

Albeit the feeling is sincere.

BETWEEN A LAUGH
AND A TEAR

I'm between a laugh and a tear
Which leaves me to declare,
I do not know
Where it is I am to go.
I'm between a fire and a flame
Which leaves me confused on who to blame,
And trying to discover
How it is I'm supposed to recover.

A.A. Winston

CLASSIC

Classic tears are rolling down your face.

It's not the words.

It's the way it was said.

If you weren't such a romantic,

We'd be okay.

You have the classic smile.

The one that is saying one thing,

While exercising another right.

Growth

DEFINITION, PLEASE

I wish that I could be there
Right inside your head.
Then that way I can explain
What it is you mean.

A.A. Winston

THIS CLOSE

I just push things to the side
Trying to figure out why.
As if anyone cared
I keep coming up shy.

Growth

FAMILY

Sisters and Brothers
Are singing a song.
Sisters and Brothers
They just don't belong.
Sisters and Brothers
Is there something wrong?
Sisters and Brothers
Are the nights that long?

A.A. Winston

CLOUDS WITHIN THE MIND

I can't explain this indecision.

But I'm worried about some sort of precision.

Vacillating between me

And what others want me to be.

The thing making it hard for me to see.

When it becomes clear

What I should hold dear.

Without receiving another's sneer,

I will be protected from all my fears.

Growth

SUNBEAM

There's a sunbeam somewhere.
I'm looking for it so desperately.
Despite all my efforts
I can't find it anywhere.
Like a ray of hope
It must appear,
From any direction
To any shore.

A.A. Winston

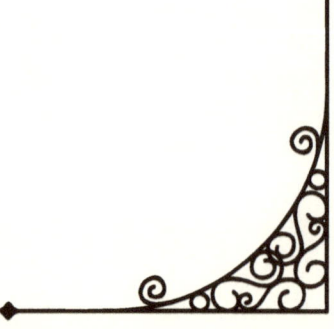

DON'T LOSE SLEEP

Now I'm really sad to see you go
And I really, really don't even know
If I should let it show.

Now I really have something to share
But I can't tell if you care
And you're the only one who can allay my fear.
I've been dancing with this thought in my mind
I'm not really sure if I should give it the time.

If I felt I could refrain
I would insist you remain
'Cause only you can free me from this pain.

So easily I could lose sight
Of what would be considered right
But I won't walk away without a fight.

Now I really think this should be said
That I truly value you as a friend
If that is the way, it's to end.

I doubt it, but if you are,
Don't lay awake too long.

Growth

SELF-PITY

We've all felt the heartache.
We've all felt the pain.
No sense feeling sorry for yourself
When everyone else has to feel it for you.

A.A. Winston

EXHAUSTION, PART I

My eyes are tired

As my soul sags.

My heart hangs

As low as a bottomless hole.

My head has stopped spinning

For it has been twisted in too many directions.

My lie I live by

Has rendered me senseless.

Growth

EXHAUSTION, PART II

I'm tired of people.
People are tired of me.
There's no need to go on
Except in solitary.

A.A. Winston

UNACHIEVABLE

Out of all the dreams
I pick one thing to be.
The one thing
Which can't be achieved.

Growth

BASEBALL

A.A. Winston

They say it's boring,

But not to me.

They just don't understand the concept.

The skills involved are hard to achieve.

Hard work and a dream

Make it worthwhile.

It relaxes the most complex of minds,

It tans the lightest of skins.

A party of strangers become brothers

Who lose their cares and animosities to the warmth.

The tradition speaks for itself.

The history stands alone.

Stories are many and quite varied.

The game has character along with characters.

From Fenway to Chavez Ravine,

Many memories have been accumulated.

And one more thing this great game has to offer,

The Fenway Frank!

GET IT STRAIGHT!

What's wrong with you?
Is there some sort of problem?
Why can't you get it straight?

Why are you pushing yourself?
Just relax.
Don't think of result Before piecing it together?
Take your own advice—
Be calm and cool!

Or could it be your over-confident?
If it is, then beware!
You can't go far
Always thinking you're the best!

You have the skills and know-how.
Leave the mind games to the shrinks.
Take it slow!
Let it flow!
Then maybe you can get it straight!

Growth

THE PREDICAMENT

Life is but a puzzle
And many pieces need to be put in place.
When one doesn't fit
Another may be tried.
The solutions are few and hidden
And not always traceable.
Someday, though, the pieces will fall into place.
Only then will the puzzle be legible.

A.A. Winston

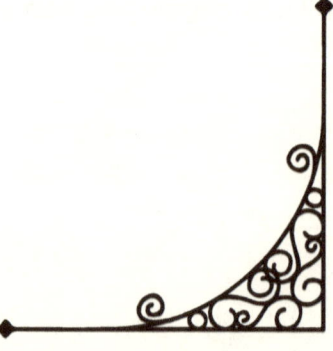

METHODS

What does it take to be #1?

Are there rules or certain regulations?

Read carefully and you shall see.

Confidence and cunning,

Earn many points.

Independence with control,

Makes them look twice.

Perseverance and posture,

Please most perfectionists.

Don't forget attitude.

Play with the team,

Soon you'll be in the lineup.

Say yes when you want to say no,

And agree when you want to disagree.

This method is most appreciated

And most widely accepted.

Don't get down if these demands can't be met.

Just make up your own methods!

Growth

SPEAK TO ME

A.A. Winston

Speak to me.
Talk to me.
I want to know, I need to know
What's on your mind!
The wheels are turning
I can tell by the expression in your eyes.
What's up besides the sky?
It can't be nothing
Because even that is something.
Speak to me now
Or speak to me later
For I will always be there
In your time of need.

NATURALLY

The trees

Seemingly insignificant.

The birds

Singing their descant.

The bees

Leaning on diligence.

Too much in reality.

Forgive me for not being able to see

How it is I came to be.

Growth

FORGET THEM NOT

Take the cigar box off the shelf.

Remove the photographs from the box.

Open the chest up in the attic.

Don't complain of what is not

Remember the memories you have got.

A.A. Winston

THE NEIGHBORHOOD

What a beautiful day in the neighborhood!
Time to think of the bad,
But don't forget the good.

Won't you be my friend?
'Cause if yes is your answer
Then the world won't come to an end.

Can't you be my neighbor?
If you move next door
You can borrow a cup of my sugar.

Mr. Rogers will have nothing on us.
We can talk over the fence
Find lots of topics to discuss.

Growth

TAKING STOCK

I love being with you.
I love sharing with you.
I love caring for you.
But no promises today.
And I don't feel the need
To restock the shelves.

A.A. Winston

MOTHER AND SON

Momma, this is your son.

Momma, where has it all gone?

I remember my kindergarten days

Your volunteering ways.

Growing up, growing apart.

Why can't we go back to the start?

If blood were water

We would be drought stricken.

Our passions race on separate tracks

Focusing on not getting distracted

While we drift from where we want to stay

Constantly watching what we say.

I would like to reclaim

The closeness we once had.

I would like to reclaim

The love shared by mother and son.

Growth

INTOXICATION

You're a hazard to my health.
The one I endear.

You're my nicotene,
My line of cocaine.
Give me a little.
Make me beg for more.

Give me more!
Give me more!

See me shaking.
See me sweat.
Say so long to sobriety.
I need the fix one more time.

A.A. Winston

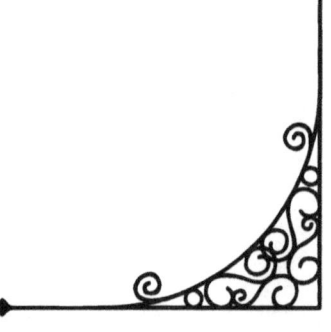

HEROES OF OUR TIME

All rolled up in a ball

With not much more that a ragged overcoat.

Wandering the streets

With everyday hopes of finding something to eat.

Looking in the faces of total strangers

Those who believe they are part of the danger.

The heroes of our time

Lay sleeping in alley ways

Waking on front staircases

Giving the rich an excuse to feel poor.

Growth

THE END

A.A. Winston

It takes time for me, takes time for you
It was long and sometimes bitter
If we had better communication,
We could have lasted a lifetime.

But it's over now,
Nothing can stop it,
We can't go back,
This is the end.

Decisions were to be made
By me, by you
And we made the ones we thought were right.
They were in our best interest, and there's no backing down.

'Cause it's over now,
Nothing can stop it,
We can't go back,
This is the end.

Starting over with new people can be so hard
But is something that has to be done
We have to accept our new endeavors,
We are embarking on a new beginning.

Seeing each other with other people will hurt for a while
But the hurting stops, and it becomes easier
Pain and hurt are the things that make experiences.
For now, let's hold on to our memories and go on.

'Cause it's over now,
Nothing can stop it,
We can't go back,
This is the end.

Growth

IT'S OVER

A.A. Winston

When you told me I thought it untrue.
You said goodbye with no reason at hand.
I tried to understand but couldn't,
As you said it's over.

We agreed to be friends.
I didn't think it would work.
It's been up and down,
Ever since you said it's over.

That day I thought I had a chance.
You were kind and receptive.
But when I went to your house later
You ignored me once again.
I still don't know what the problem was
Or why you had to say it's over.

PASSION

Passion—

I kiss your lips.

Passion—

I caress your breasts.

Passion—

I massage your loins.

Passion—

I move deep into you.

Passion—

I release into you.

Passion.

Growth

ONE STEP AWAY

We've been one step away
For so long.
I can hardly believe
It won't come true.

There's been a lot of pain
Involved in my pleasure.
You've been the inspiration
To portions of my frustrations.

You've had the chances
As I sat with bated breath.
Call me today
Let me be with you.

The carrot has dangled
Over my head.
Like Bacchus at the grapevine
I can't quite get a grasp.

So close,
That's you and me.
May—September
Have it your way.

A.A. Winston

How do we resolve
The questions of our minds?
Our hearts always meet
But our heads still separate.

Our faces tell the story
That everyone reads.
One more step
Would be a step too far.

Growth

CRYING FOR LOVE

I never had to cry for love,
But here I am sitting all alone.
Somehow, I've lost my way.
It's been so easy to find
Yet so hard to hang onto.

I never had to beg for love,
But without you I am a lonesome dove.
Flying about hoping to find my peace
Wondering what it will take.

I never had to chase love,
But would the love be futile without the chase?
Will I appreciate it less?
Maybe so or maybe no.

But please forgive me,
I never had to cry for love.

A.A. Winston

FIRST RHYME

Once while sitting and staring

I thought of a word
While at the same time as being bored.
Then I thought that rhymes with sword,
Which rhymes with fjord,
Which rhymes with cord,
Which rhymes with Ford
Which rhymes with hoard,
Which rhymes with soared...

Why stop?
Many more words rhyme with bored.
Like moored,
And roared,
Which in turn rhymes with poured,
Which rhymes with toured,
Which somehow rhymes with scored,
Which, if need be, rhymes with...

Hey wait!
I get the feeling I'm being ignored.

Growth

YOUR TURN TO FINISH

People knowing things unknown
Tend to make the most of everything.
Feeble jealousies supplant rationale,
Stripping man of all his pride.
The last word is always sought...

A.A. Winston

THE HEART IS HOME

Here is something to keep you warm

Through those cold nights.

If the mind,

Or the body,

Should chill just a bit,

May this be your first layer.

This will enable me to be

Next to your warmest part

And that is, of course, your heart!

Growth

A SHIFT IN WEIGHT

For so long it has been the same,
Many follows one.
A shift is imminent.
The opinions of the many
Outweigh the opinion of one.
The voices in the crowd are now being heard.
No matter how bad, it is for the best,
Just so the right ears are to the ground.

A.A. Winston

IMAGES

So many images.

Some so vivid.

Others too ambiguous.

Many quite deceiving.

Dream-like images

Just out of reach.

Fantasies of the mind Intangible to the eyes.

Realistic images

Wishing they would disappear.

Closing the eyes to get away

Produces more of the things you try to escape—

Images.

Growth

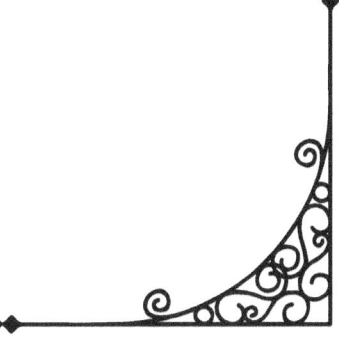

FALSE CONCEIT

A.A. Winston

When everything is said and done
We look back.
There are no traces of tomorrow
Just memories of yesterday.

The mirror reflects the beast
And hides the beauty.
A combination of extremes
We hate to admit.

Pummeled by fate
That we chose to create.
Forget the circumstances
And pay the price.

Unfortunate happenings
You cannot deny.
Follow the trail
For the path reveals
How we often fail.

TIME TO COME HOME

When things get bad
And you're tired of picking yourself up,
It is probably time to come home.

Beating your head against the wall
Forces bleeding but does not help.
When it's hard to figure out how it will work
Then maybe it's time to come home.

When everything you try
Seems to go awry,
You begin to think it's time to come home.

When everybody says yes
And it always turns out no
The realities overcome the doubts
And you definitely know,
it's time to come home.

Growth

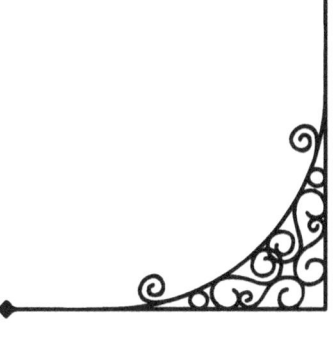

THE WANTING OF A WISH

A.A. Winston

I turned around and there she stood
Without knowledge, without a clue.
Her sweet smile
Brought daylight
To what otherwise would have been
A night of unfulfilled dreams.
The spark of her eyes
Set fire to my heart.
She looked aimlessly into the darkness
Her thoughts never to be told.
What innocence does she possess?
This fact is unknown
But gives me a feeling of hope!
If ever I wanted a wish
I would wish to be with you!

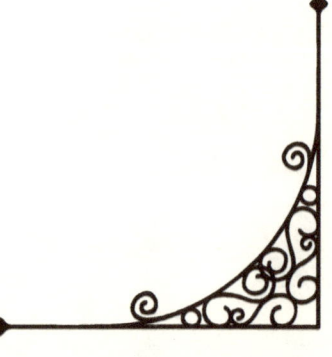

CITY LIGHTS

I see the lights
Over the city.
They shine so bright
Like the hope of tomorrow.

I see the lights
Over the city.
They take me away
To thoughts of you.

These are good thoughts.
These are bad thoughts.
But they make it all worthwhile.
They make the world spin 'round.

There are no dark ages
In the sparkle of your eyes.
You kindle the fire
That burns deep inside.

I see the lights
Over the city.
They shine so bright
Like the hope of tomorrow.

Growth

Roaming roads of the mind
Searching for the direction home.
Lost the desire
Not the hope.

Seeing straight is sometimes a problem
Until I focus on you.
Then it's all too clear
So clear it's scary.

I see the lights
Over the city.
They take me away
To thoughts of you.

I see the lights
Over the city.
They shine so bright
Like the hope of tomorrow.

A.A. Winston

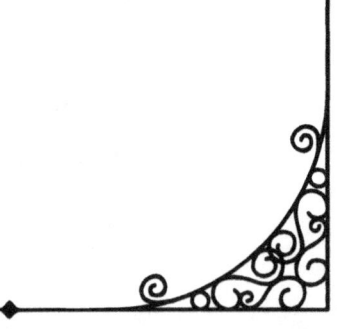

PRIDE AND RESPECT

Pride is your solace.

A something that can't be taken away

Only damaged.

Nobody can strip it from you

Unless permitted.

If pride is lost,

So goes dignity and confidence.

Smeared integrity

Severs pride

But doesn't kill it.

It is ever present.

To regain,

Take control,

Reassert yourself,

Show what your made of,

Show them your back.

Do the pushing,

Don't be pushed.

Demand respect

And respect will follow.

The time is now,

The time is right.

Growth

VISIONS

A.A. Winston

Looking behind closed doors.
Peering through rose-colored glasses.

Hidden.
Lost.
Untraceable.

What you don't think is there
Can be found.
It all depends on where you look.

When I open those closed doors,
And remove those rose-colored glasses from my eyes,
What do you suppose I see?
I see the shadows that surround you.

I see nothing.
Nothing but you.

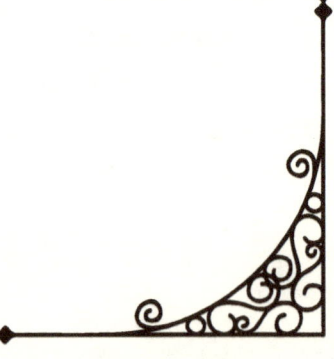

A PAPER MIND

Certain words are hard for me
Mainly the important ones.
I cannot say them in any other way
But pieced together in phrases on paper.
The truth of emotion lies in my soul,
Seeking a release or collapse.
Coolness of nature soothes my inner heat.
With unknown passion my conviction strives.

Growth

DOUBLE TAKE

There is one thing you wouldn't think I would be.

That one thing is a poet,

Because I don't really show it.

I usually don't rhyme,

But give me time.

Just a few bugs to work out.

Don't worry, I won't sit and pout.

This revelation is probably a surprise,

I can see it in your eyes.

Please don't let this change us,

And please don't make a big fuss.

I wrote this for you

So don't sue.

I just want you to know

That you are the sun

And you make this world a lot more fun.

A.A. Winston

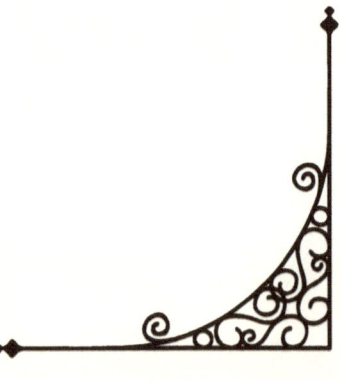

THE PERSON WITHIN

The pounding of the heart can be so loud.

Trying to break free

The boundaries are endless.

Expressing your feelings receives criticism, nonetheless.

Good or bad no one really understands.

Your ideas are good while his ideas are great.

Good ideas always work,

The great ones just die out.

Listen to what is being said

The voice you hear is your own.

Growth

FORTUNES OF LIFE

A.A. Winston

They are the things we strive for.
The things we desire.
And what we sometimes live for.
They are the fortunes of life.

Dreams are made of these.
At times unreachable
But certainly not inconceivable.
These are the fortunes of life.

When our eyes are closed
This is what we envision.
Good always conquers evil.
This is the fortune of life.

Many do the asking,
Some get the receiving,
But only the ones who truly deserve, get,
The fortunes of life.

Working hard to go the distance.
Not stopping when someone says no
Can only provide
The fortunes of life.

There is no end.
There is no beginning.
There is always the wanting
Of the fortunes of life.

Growth

THE BURNING FIRE

Pen to paper
Could flint the fire
Burn holes in everyone's soul.
What does it matter?
Nobody cares to read the ink,
Or dare to print the stink.

A.A. Winston

RECORDED LINES

In this "Land of Confusion"
Never let the "Freedom Overspill."
Always remember there will be "Finer Things"
When that "Higher Love" arrives.
You may have to make a "Split Decision" or two
But you must "Take It as It Comes."
"Angels Never Call."
"My Love is Leavin'"
Though not on "Judgement Day."
When I return
Hope will remain
That it will bring you
"Back To the High Life" again.

Growth

YA KNOW?

What do you think of this world?

It's like screwed, ya know?

Elaborate a little.

Ya know like the world is starving.
And countries are fighting, ya know?
 Like what are we doing?
Throwing it all away, ya know?
Whatever happened to talking?
Take it from me,
Good communication is key, ya know?
Ya know where I'm coming from?
If I were president my speeches would relate, ya know?
Ya know, simple and easy to understand.
That's what we need, ya know?
No more war heads,
Just more thinking heads, ya know?

A.A. Winston

ALPHABET COUPLETS I

Standing around with nothing to do.

Splitting hairs seems like fun.

Wondering where the sun comes from,

Wishing it could last so long.

Pondering decisions of the heart,

Placing doubts in the mind.

Open to certain suggestions,

Offered by so many souls.

Noticing things otherwise unseen,

Nothing comes to light but darkness.

Turning the pages of a book,

Trying hard to comprehend.

Running nowhere too fast,

Relying on inner instincts.

Questioning the hands of time,

Quietly sitting by the wayside.

Yawning when things get boring,

Yearning for some sort of desire.

Driving with the headlights off,

Daring fate and taking a chance.

Eastern winds from the west,

Echoing loudly in the distance.

Hearing lies around the corner,

Growth

Hidden people stand behind.
Visions of something stuck inside,
Vying for top spot in importance.
Missing persons with missing minds,
Meandering along some unknown path.

A.A. Winston

ALPHABET COUPLETS II

Manipulating words of man,

Meaning nothing of significance.

Fanciful in fashion,

Forever unchanging.

Ahead of time,

Away from the crowd.

Indigenous to humanity,

Insistent on things unknown.

Getting out of bed for no reason,

Given wisdom not of the wise.

Jokingly living life,

Jabbing into a black hole.

Zipping about,

Zealous to the needs.

Undetected as is invisible,

United as we fall.

Clones of each other,

Cornered by the pressures.

Behind the closed doors,

Beckons the sound of a hollow light.

Looking deep into the soul,

Leaving nothing but the fingerprints.

Kin all around,

Keeping us silent.

Growth

A SUBTLE DEPENDENCY

A.A. Winston

When I'm lonely
I look upon you to see me through.
When I'm sad
I'd like to have you here.
When I'm mad
I'd like you to be on my side.

When I'm lost without a trace
I'd like to see you on the case.
When I need someone who cares
I'd like to see you there.
When I think of who I love
I will always think of you.

You tug at me
Like no one ever could.
Your positive ideals
Whisk away the fears.
A tender smile
Removes the doubts.

The subtle touches
Strengthen the happiness.
You provide the simplest of pleasures
Only known to all of man.

CONTINUED MATURITY

We all go through different stages in life. New experiences – good, bad, indifferent – make us who we are as we age. We start out young and impressionable.

We move toward a more enlightened station in life as we move into young adulthood. We then progress, if we continue to learn, to realizations and impressions shaped through a variety of interactions and relationships – both direct and indirect.

In the third book of this series, the 75 poems in **Continued Maturity** includes writings of a man moving toward and into middle age. He's lived through successful failures, burned by idealism and naivete. They are reflections of creeping jade and cynicism. The battle, however, to believe continues.

Continued Maturity is the third phase, most likely not the last, of a person's life that I hope others may relate.

Growth

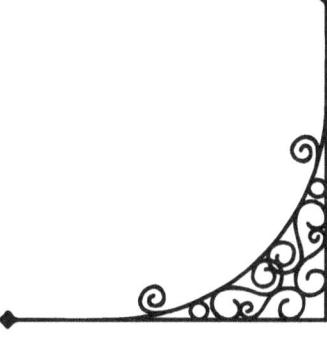

BETCHA CAN'T

You say you can do things better.
I betcha can't!
Whining and bickering like a little kid.
You'll never see me act that way.
I'm too mature,
Much too grown up.
The competition is too much for you
And you'll never reach my level.
So, whenever you say you can,
I will be there to say betcha can't!

A.A. Winston

KAT-MAN-DO

What the kat man says
The kat man do!
The kat man can do anything.

He is the maker of dreams.
He pulls the rabbit out of the hat.
He can make illusions seem real.

His stories transfix.
His eyes mesmerize.
His gestures tantalize.
He makes you believe in something
Which can't be true.

Growth

He chooses not to lose,
Although he never could.
He has spring in his step
And vigor in his voice.

He is a winner.
He is a champ.
For an example of what we can do,
Just look at kat-man-do.

SILENT SOUND

Are you around,
To hear my sound?
If so,
Why not call?
What a feeling
When no one is there.
And to be in a room
Where even the walls
Have no ears.

A.A. Winston

THE VIEW

Why can't life be this clear?
Seeing forever,
As though looking in a crystal ball.
Blue skies as far as I can see.
Everything looks so rosy.
The beauty seems to stretch to eternity,
And the miles seem forever distant.

The view,
It is a little thing
That makes me appreciate the big things.
In its simplicity
It goes a long way.

Growth

AHEAD OF THE TIMES

A.A. Winston

Push, shove
Any way to get ahead.

Possessions, obsessions
Anything to get ahead.

Control, hoard
To be ahead.

Hook, crook
Any how to stay ahead.

Con, pawn
Some way to stay ahead.

Cunning, running
It's all in the head.

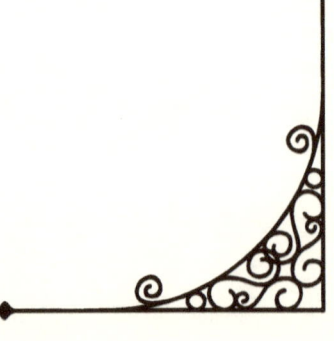

THE RIGHT OF THE WRONG

Everybody has a voice
That beckons from the inside.
Everybody speaks despite not being heard.

The good ideas are often overlooked
Passed up for something "better."
The worst usually becomes the best.

Criticisms fly past the eyes
And brought out in public,
Only to cause speculation.
That is the right of the wrong.

Hollow heads always hear
But never retain.
Others keep while the rest sleep.

No matter what is said
Someone has to be upset.
That is the right of the wrong.

Growth

SANCTUARY

Look around,
Nowhere to be found.
Your search has led to everywhere,
Yet to turn up a thing.
Look closer at the things that surround you.
Can you find it now?
It could be under your nose.
Someplace you wouldn't expect.
It may be on the inside.
Don't give up,
Keep up the search!
Someday it will find you.
Sooner or later, you will discover
Your own sanctuary.

A.A. Winston

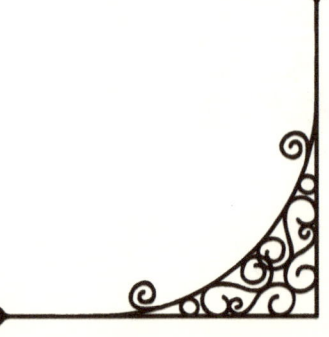

THE ACHIEVEMENT

Striving for the crowning moment
Waiting in the wings for the big step
Hearing rumors, it may happen soon
Knowing time is your ally
Contemplating wrong or right
Closing in on the deadline
Wishing for the desired decision.
The time has come, and you have won.
People leap in congratulations.
Suddenly the dream is over.
The morning after can be so cruel.

Growth

THE NIGHT WITHOUT CLUTTER

A.A. Winston

Twas' the night before Pueblo
And all through the studios
Not a soul was searching,
Only a man named Pete
And his high-powered soundboard.
While he played his songs
A sound of much clutter was heard.
He exclaimed, "what could this be?"
It could not be the wind
For the night was quite calm.
The man states, "maybe my mind is playing tricks on me."
Until finally he sees the light.
Of course, it could be nothing but
The ghosts of clutter free pasts
Sending messages to their successors.
As the ghosts have gone away
An encouraging word was heard,
"A good evening to all,
And to all a clut-ter free night."

FRAILTY

Believe it or not
This comes from the heart.
And here is to the hope
That we last longer
Than the life of a rose.

Growth

THE FREEDOM WRINGS

One always hears
In the music we tune to
That the male and female alike
Aren't happy without each other.
But why do they complain?
If they didn't want to live apart,
Then why did they break it off!
This is too much of a resounding sound.
Before hooking up one always praises,
When together each other curses.
Why not let it rest?
Start from scratch,
Sit back and relax!
And let the freedom wring!

A.A. Winston

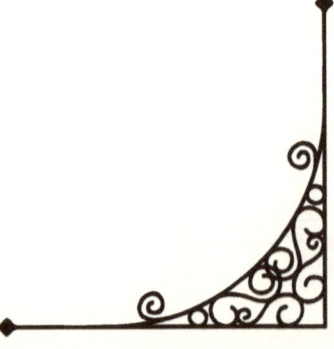

GRAPHICALLY SPEAKING

Everything is written on paper
But nothing is being said.
Things which are apparent
Aren't always inevitable.
Etchings create a picture
Never showing but one side.

I STILL BELIEVE

I still believe
In what I see.
I still believe
In what I can be.
I still believe
In what we can lead.
I still believe
We should be freed.
I still believe
In our every need.
But most of all I still believe
That together we can live happily indeed.

A.A. Winston

SHADED FATE

My cries of hurt are being heard,

Only in secluded passages.

It is me who is the one to speak.

The hands of fate cannot twist my aim.

My future of promise

Has darkened under the bright lights.

THE VOICE

A voice cried out

I knew it well.

I've heard it many times before.

It seems to be following me

To wherever I may go.

I'm afraid of it,

And it knows this all too well.

When I fail it speaks to me,

When I succeed it whispers in my ear.

I can't avoid it.

It is everywhere.

As a matter of fact, I hear it calling now.

I hear the voice of fear.

A.A. Winston

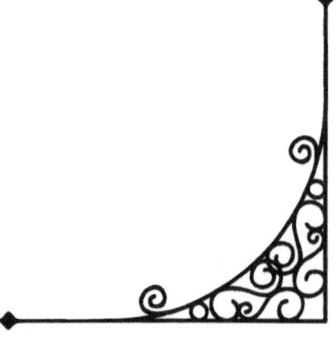

RENAISSANCE MAN

He's a genius of a time
He could never realize.
A throwback to the future
Uncontrollably bound in the present.

Growth

THE REVELATION

What you see may not always be real.

It could be some kind of illusion.

There is a mask upon it,

Holding out for the surprise,

Nobody would think of it,

Maybe nobody cares.

But it's gone on for a year,

And it's reached its pinnacle.

Nobody knew,

Except for a minimal few.

Now everyone will know,

But as far as I'm concerned,

What's in a name?

Two s's, two l's and three d's.

A.A. Winston

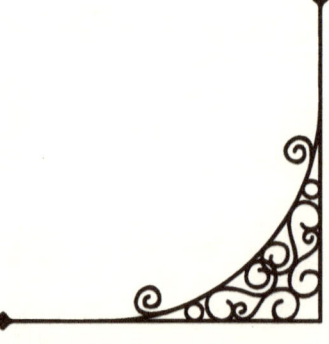

TRANSLATION

Yes, I'm pissed!
How could you tell?
It is quite obvious, isn't it?
My troubles are written
In five different languages
All over this sad and sorry face.

Growth

THE ROPES

Climbing the ladder
Striving for success,
There is usually someone to show you the ropes.
When in trouble,
Wrap the ropes around your waist.
Secure what was learned
And never forget.
Refer to the ropes whenever possible.
They are what solutions are made of.

A.A. Winston

SCREAMS ON THE INSIDE

Listen to how I feel.

The message can't be any clearer.

Clues are strategically placed

Just waiting for you to notice.

Your busy work life

And active social life

Are above all your main priorities.

Who am I to say I don't understand?

I see it in the papers.

I see it on the streets.

I wonder how it feels.

I picture me.

Nooses are too hard to tie.

Pills are hard to swallow.

Slashing my wrists would be too messy.

And guns make it too final.

Growth

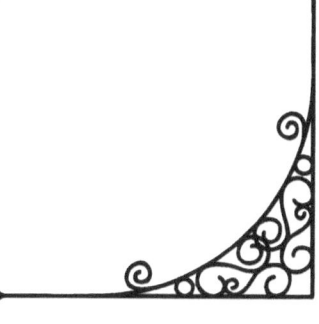

Are these just excuses?
Won't someone hear my screams?
The pressure is too much,
The pain unbearable.

To my friends, I leave my possessions.
To my enemies, contentment.
And to my family, my love and memory.

A.A. Winston

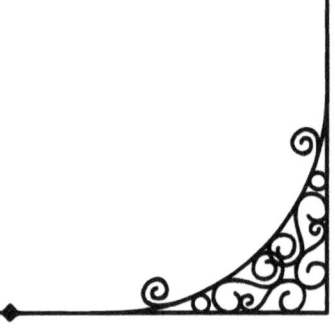

DERANGEMENT

Playing with your mind like Russian roulette

Pushing up daisies while singing the blues

Them are just some things I can't explain.

You're a dizzy demon in disguise

Pulling strings, having no heed.

Sounds like a guitar with a strange melody.

Waiting for someone else to come along

Hoping for someone who will give you what you want.

Confusion and deception are everything and its

The thing that gives you strength.

Many don't see it, but the lucky ones do.

You may think you have control but then

Somehow it slips away.

Only the strong-willed can fight you

And they will most likely spread the word.

I can't help feeling sorry while feeling good too,

Because you'll soon be part of everyone's past.

Growth

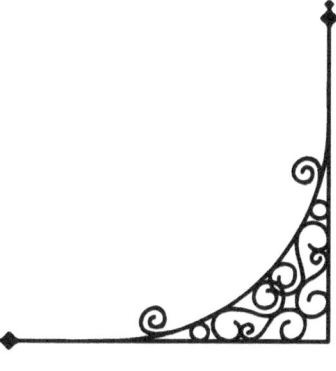

TRIVIAL II

A.A. Winston

Broken fingernails,
Such distress!
Smeared mascara, such a sin!
Shoes don't match dress,
Burn at the stake!
Hair is a mess,
Put a hat on!
Why go to extremes?
The thing we appreciate is the masterpiece,
Without the paint.
Just the canvas.
The person underneath
Is all that matters.
Masks are not needed
For they hide the true self.
Trivial incidents make me wonder,
Why be someone else
When you can be yourself?

BLUE

Time ran out.
Patience did too.
No job.
No money.
No sense holding on.

Great potential at the start
Sputtered to a halt.
Recycling the excitement
Took too many resources.
Replaced by routine
Burned out on being with you.

I don't have any great qualms.
Joyous and fun were our times
But none to sustain substantial ties.
I figured this was it
And led you to believe it too.
I didn't think I'd be sitting here
Waiting to hang up on the line.

Growth

I wish there was an easier way
But my mind is unclear
With the distress this will create.
Unfortunately, I fear this is only right.

Goodbye and I am in your debt.
Hanging with me is something few people can take.
I feel sorry I could not give to you
What you still want to give to me.

Farewell, my love
For that will never die
I said it once
And in your memories can rely.

A.A. Winston

TION'ED

Undivided attention
Just brings retention.
There's no such thing as fascination
Just hallucination.
Grim determination
Breeds isolation.
One's conviction
Is another's insurrection.

Growth

STRAIN OF THE HEART

A.A. Winston

You say you're searching,
For what, I don't know.
I ask you to look in my eyes
But you say they provide no light.

I ask you to take my hand
But you insist that it is too weak.
You pull the strings of my heart
And only dissonance is heard.

It pains me to see you this way
But all I can do is obey what you say.
The help I want to give
Is not the help you want.

The pleasure and pain are always there.
The strain of the heart is what you get.

The stake has been put in place
And it feels there is room to go deeper.
The hammer is about to hit
As you decide to halt.

Please follow me,
Maybe you will see
Through some sort of vision
That I'm not such a threat.
You profess you know what it's like
And say I've never been through the experience.
Before it comes to an all too sudden end
Check to see who was unwilling to bend.

The pleasure and pain are always there.
The strain of the heart is what you get.

Growth

THE DEVIL

A menace to many
A tragedy in someone else's mind.
He's the bright light in everyone's dark room
The emotional fortress we all hide in,
He cures whatever ails
Despite what is believed.
He's the fun side of God
Or maybe just God.

A.A. Winston

I SAY ONE

Life may not always give you what you want,
But I can take it—
It's better than being dead.

JUST A QUIP

Don't worry—
I'm just like everybody else—
I start the day sleeping too.

A.A. Winston

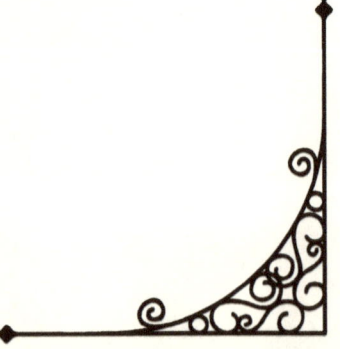

HUNGER

Tanks and guns
Are not the real weapons.
Minds and money make all the moves.
Pressing a button means much more
Than protecting a people from dying out.

Growth

FOR REAL

A.A. Winston

Surreal, Surreal, Surreal!
I'm looking for Surreal!
Have you seen Surreal?
He has to be somewhere.
I just don't understand.
I've seen the Blahs,
They're doing well.
Excitement is such the nomad.
But I really need to speak
To that man named Surreal.
His cousin Eclectic said I could find him here.
I guess I'll just sit and wait
For something real.
Because Surreal seems so unreal.

WHAT A CLICHÉ!

I'm tired of all the same old cliches

Passing off as creativity.

The same old words reaching for new meaning.

A state of laziness has us all mesmerized.

Our eyes are closed,

The flame of ingenuity burned out.

Now I can see

How easy it can be

To keep saying the same stupid things!

Growth

HEADACHE

Stop talking!
I don't need to hear it.
Constant complaints
Give me constant cerebral tension.
Whatever you say
Has passed over my brain twice over.
No need to go on.
I've given myself... A headache.

A.A. Winston

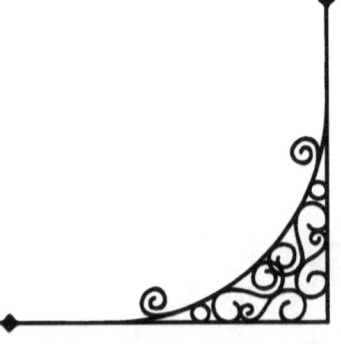

A TIP OF THE GLASS

Here's to the future...
For it is like a glass.
 It could be full
Or it could be empty,
Depending on your life choices.

Growth

SINK OR SWIM

Peace, safety, and happiness
Are all shores I cannot reach.
Just think—If I could swim
What life would be like.

A.A. Winston

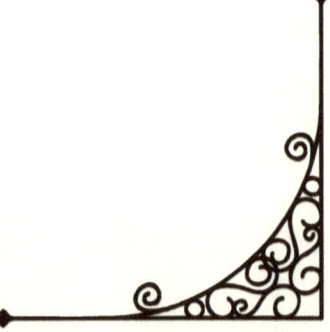

JUST HANGIN'

When things appear inconclusive
I can't bring myself
To just hang around.
Little can be brought to fruition
When nothing can be found.

Growth

A FIGURE

It's just a figure of speech
When I say, "I don't mean to preach."
How can I pray when I
Don't believe in what I say?

SUNSET, SUNRISE

Sitting face to face

Against the sun

With nothing to say

Just something to contemplate.

When the sun sets

It will be time to leave.

Before it rises once again

We must find what was lost.

If unable to,

We will never return.

Growth

REVENGE

Revenge is sweeter than people think.
Some say don't get mad.
I can't see how that can stimulate.
The intensity of equaling the score
Can be so satisfying.
Forget walking away
Get even and walk free.

A.A. Winston

QUIET, PLEASE

Shut up!
Shut up!
Just shut your fucking face!

Shut up!
Shut up!
I can't take you anymore!

Shut up!
Shut up!
The sound is very grating!
Your voice is becoming really grating!

So, shut up!

Growth

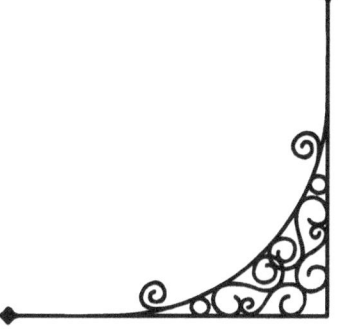

MY GENERATION

This is my generation.
The products of failure.
Failed education.
Failed jobs.
Failed government.
Failed parents.

This is my generation.
Scared of the future.
Afraid the past will catch up.
This is my generation.
Stuck behind a "me" generation.
Ahead of a "know-nothing" generation.
Part of a betrayed generation.

This is my generation.
Keeper of the burden.
No thanks from anyone.
No one's shoulder to put it on.

This is my generation.
Give us the map
So we can find our way out.

A.A. Winston

THE NOTICE

Look at me!
Look at me!
I am the forgotten one.
I am not gone, though.
Yet should I be?

MARCHING ON

Though I put my feelings on parade—
And it seems like an act of desperation—
Don't be surprised to see me again—
Somewhere deep into the night.

A.A. Winston

THE BALANCING ACT

Put your heart on the line.
Don't be afraid.
You're no Wallenda.
So I can be your net.

SHHH!

Silence is golden
When you do what you're told.
That's not always possible.
But it keeps you from good trouble.

A.A. Winston

NO GAME

Roulette with a Russian accent
Is a game I don't want to play.
So, stop making believe
That everything is okay.

Growth

HOW FAR WE'VE COME?

They sit in L.A.
They wait in L.A.
They riot in L.A.
They burn in L.A.
They die in L.A.

They sit in the U.S.A.
They wait in the U.S.A.
They riot in the U.S.A.
They burn in the U.S.A.
They die in the U.S.A.
They sit in D.C.

They riot in L.A.
They sit in D.C.
They burn in L.A.
They sit in D.C.
They die in L.A.

They die in L.A.
They die in L.A.
They die in L.A.

A.A. Winston

INNOCENCE

I'm innocent!
At least I want to be.
But I haven't been
Since I was twelve—
Standing over my father's grave.

Growth

I SAY TWO

Give a little love
You gotta live to learn.

A.A. Winston

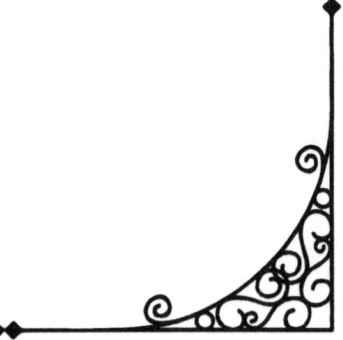

OVER THE SHOULDER

I didn't see you coming
In the rear-view mirror.
Like a flashback
You popped in my head.
Like a shadow
It was never everlasting.
I walk the line
With much futility,
And even more despair.

Growth

ME, SORRY?

I never said that I was sorry,
And I probably never will.
It's a shame we came to this.
The loss of language led to worry.
And soon thereafter a departure.
The blame rests on our shoulders.
Despite what you believe.

A.A. Winston

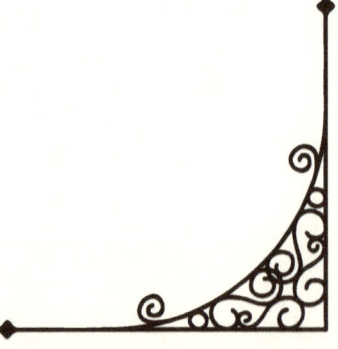

YOU

And I realized

You are the only woman for me

You can handle my flaws

You can cope with my insecurities

You understand how I work

How I think

How I need

Deal with my idiosyncrasies

Discourage my obscurities

You are my true relevancy

My better reality

And I realized

You are the only woman for me.

Growth

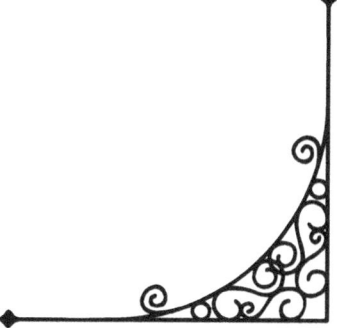

FUEL-FILLMENT

A.A. Winston

You fuel my hopes
You fuel my dreams
You fuel my desires.

I've fallen on the sword so many times
For so many people
Sacrificing my wants and needs
At times losing track of who I am.

You fill my hopes
You fill my dreams
You fill my desires.

Stick with me
Stay with me
Promise to always be there.

Be there when the sun rises
Be there when the sun sets
When we say goodnight
The stars climb to new heights.

Be there when I turn around
Always have my back
Always guide me to stay out front.

I will stick with you
I will stay with you
I promise to always be there.

You fuel my hopes
You fuel my dreams
You fuel my desires.

You fill my hopes
You fill my dreams
You fill my desires.

I will be there when the sun rises
I will be there when the sun sets
When we say goodnight
The stars climb to new heights.

Growth

I will be there when you turn around
I will always have your back
I will always guide you to stay out front.

You fuel my hopes
You fuel my dreams
You fuel my desires.

You fill my hopes
You fill my dreams
You fill my desires.

F & E & A

A.A. Winston

Think of what the words mean
Forever in my heart
Ever on my mind
Always in my soul.

Many years ago
Split decisions made while we roam
The anxious hellos
The lingering goodbyes
Resolve was where our hearts laid.

Damage done
Missed opportunities left behind
Wounds leave deep scars
Forever in my heart
Ever on my mind
Always in my soul.

Eight letters
Three words
One meaning
Is the only description
Perhaps the best prescription.

SOBER DRUNKENNESS

I can't get drunk tonight
It only makes me miss you more
It's a sobering effect
To only touch you by text
Spoken words through cell wire
Just stokes my desire.

Growth

ENLIGHTENMENT

What do I need?
A partnership.
Sincerity.
Genuine caring.
Consideration.
Loyalty.
A formidable give and take.

Someone who is willing
To accept me for my flaws.
And I mean...
Really accept those flaws
For I have many.
While I never expect
Unconditional love
As I don't totally believe
There is such a thing,
I believe in sacrifice
And compromise
And two people
Working together to endure.

A.A. Winston

Around that corner
Came a dark-haired,
Grayish green-eyed wonder
With dimples
You could eat cereal out of.
An intoxicating pick-me-up
Who fatefully made contact.
One small step...

Like the first moon landing
A giant leap was taken
In my personal mankind.
Hit and miss as it may seem,
The metronome ticks in unison
Keeping perfect time.

Growth

Too often we don't see
Opportunities laying right before us.
Recognition of opportunities
Many times
Come at the hand of low points.
A spike in the midst of dips.

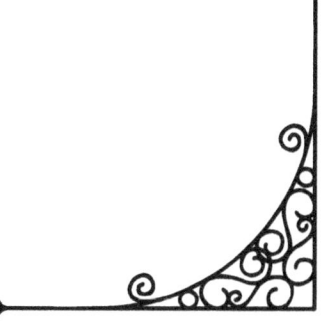

CIRCULATION

A.A. Winston

Life is circular
Goes round and round
From the beginning
We keep returning home.

People come
People go
People pass right through.

Some stay for awhile
Some toss a nod
Some come at the right time.

Life is circular
Goes round and round
Those that made the better part of you
Always return home.

THROWING WORDS TOGETHER

Ignore me when I'm down
Pick me up by my bootstraps
Bring your spark to me.

Words can't speak
But your eyes shout loudly
There is no silence in your desire.

Growth

THROWING MORE WORDS TOGETHER

I need to sleep now

I'm so tired

It's time to dream

See what life is really about

Put aside the craziness and deceit

Close my eyes and see the light

Sleep now and forever hold my peace.

A.A. Winston

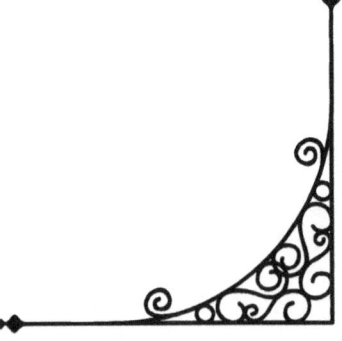

CLOSED

Closing my eyes
I see the image
Of the epitome
Finally, pieces coming together
Just a pinch closer
To find the closure.

Growth

RANDOM THOUGHT

All at once I feel overjoyed

And overwhelmed

About your presence is my life.

A.A. Winston

ANOTHER RANDOM THOUGHT

I don't have many talents
I don't have many skills
Like Popeye and his spinach
I am just what I am.

When I fall
I fall hard.
Like a tree in the forest
When no one is around.

Growth

TIME ZONE

Despite what some may think,
Despite what some may say,
True love has conditions.

Trust.
Loyalty.
Honesty.

Betrayal of one,
Betrayal of three,
Dedicated to one,
Dedicated to three.

Trust in loyalty.
Loyalty to honesty.
Honesty breeds trust.

A.A. Winston

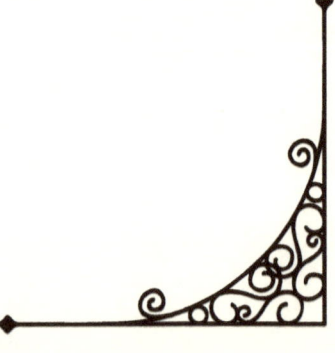

A LOT LIKE LOVE MORE

Your love
Was as everlasting
As smoke from a fire.
Wisps lifting into the air
Dissipating as it rises
Stretching apart.

Growth

GET OUTTA HERE

A.A. Winston

7:21 in the morning
I don't know where I'm going
But I'm going where I don't want to go.
I'm scared of all the disillusionment.

Clouds are rolling in
A storm is coming
Don't know if there will be shelter
When the thunder starts booming.
Waiting for a beck and call
Saving me from a fall.

I gotta get outta here
I gotta go
Too tied down
Too muffled to make a sound.

Stifled by resistance
Bound by disappointment
Tired of deception.
Bemused by the reflection.

Get me outta here
I gotta go.

GOLDEN RULE

As many of you know

I'm not the most religious

I don't wear it on my sleeve

You won't hear me quote the words

Or call out the number

But I do believe

In do unto others

As you'd like

To have done to you.

SIGHT UNSEEN

A.A. Winston

Do you see me?

I don't know

Do I see me?

Hidden in the crevices

The cracks

The holes

The places where people don't look.

Can you see me?

What do I look like?

Do I see me yet?

Heading down the pit

In the swirl of the deep.

Find me

Find me

Like a game of hide and seek.

Peek a boo

I see you

Do you want to see me?

SOMEDAY

I'm caught in the weeds
Trying to brush aside the hair from my eyes.

I cannot see what you have seen.
I cannot hear what you have heard.
I cannot feel what you have felt.
I cannot walk in your shoes.

Someday
Same place
Same space.

Growth

MOMMA CRYIN'

I hear Momma cryin'
Something bad goin' down.
I hear Momma cryin'
Sounds as loud as a train.
I hear Momma cryin'
Sirens blaring in my brain.

A.A. Winston

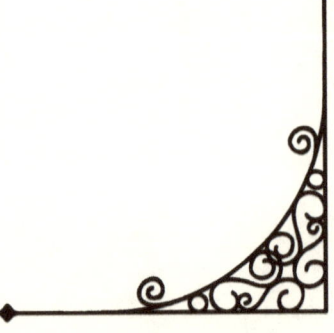

SHE WASN'T THERE
(REPULSE THIS)

I wasn't there for her
We both had our dreams divided
Our feelings for each other subsided.

Been beat up
Told to shut up
Told to believe your lies
Ratcheting up the anger and frustration.

Told to be ashamed.
That I wasn't worth a thing
Told I was repulsive
When the story tells another tale.

Many believe what you spewed
But I know the truth
I had my share of misdeeds
I didn't know about a man named Swarup.

Instead, I tossed and turned
Turned against myself
Doubted who I was
Spellbound by your myths.

Growth

I need to get this off my chest
Your deceit comes complete
With scissors and a sheath
Too bad you're not worth the shit.

The pit in my stomach
Is now a peak of my persistence
Your deeds made me replete
For it is I who can live with my existence.

I thought I lost everything
I didn't know how much I gained
I guess that was my mistake.

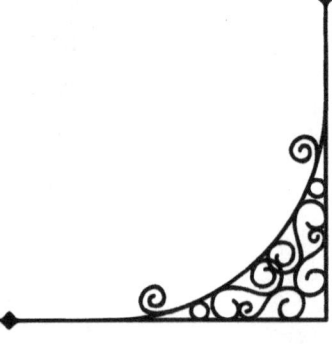

WEALTH

I'm broke
But I'm not broke.
I'm wandering
But I'm not lost.
I'm a virgin
But I'm not sexless.
I can't sing
But I still got soul.
I don't have much religion
But I still have a prayer.
I'm not a joke maker
But I have a humorous sense.
When it's time for me to stop serving
I'll know I ain't broke.

Growth

WHAT DO YOU SEE?

What do you see
In me?
That you don't see
In you?
I'm not your savior
I can't fill your gaps.

What do you see
In me?
That you don't see
In you?
Can you reflect your dreams
By deflecting them off me?
I'm not your eyes
I can't be your flame
That burns your desire.

A.A. Winston

What do you see
In me?
That you don't see
In you?
I can't write your songs
I can't swallow your doubts
That imprisons your peace.

What do you see
In me?
What don't you see
In you?
I can only add insult to your injury
Nicks to your cuts
Pricks to your psychosis.

What do you see
In me?
That you see
In you?

Growth

DON'T HOLD BACK

Don't hold back a sneeze.
Don't ignore the urge to go to the bathroom.
Don't ignore an itch.

Add a fourth – laugh out loud!

I dislike talking about myself
But anyone who knows me
Knows that
When I sneeze
I let it out
Mucous and all.

When I have to go pee
I do my best to address it.

When I have an itch
I gotta scratch it.

Lately, when something hits me funny
I am known to loudly guffaw.

Some may find that annoying
But I don't care

A.A. Winston

Because with so many things in life
We hold back
We fear the reaction of others.
We fear the opinions of others.

We are inhibited by fear
But that fear only prevents us
From exploring ideas
And thoughts
And questions
That contribute to human well-being.

If we, as a body,
Collectively practice
A kind of straight-talk discourse
Then we may be better able
To demolish inequality.

Parenthetically, there is a reason
People in power
Don't want more educated people.
But anyway, we may better eliminate
Racism
Sexism
Ageism (against both old and young)
Every-ism
And raise the level of equality
That is inclusive and participatory.

Growth

Let's embrace different thoughts
Encourage different attitudes
Exchange ideas
And share with one another
For the betterment of us.

Thus, I leave you
With something some may recognize
When we hear someone sneeze
Instead of bless you
Maybe we should say –
"You are sooo beautiful."
Thank you

A.A. Winston

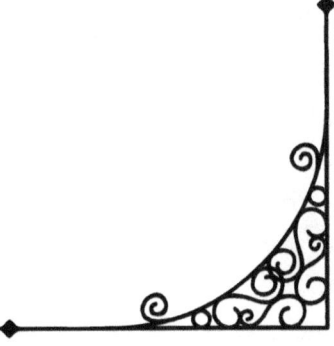

RING, RING

I came calling
Once upon a time.
The line was busy
So, I tried again.
The phone rang...
And rang and rang...
The line connected

As I started to say hello
A voice interrupted
You've reached my number
Please leave a message
At the beep...

As I paused after the beep
Another voice said...
This voice mailbox is full.
Another time
Another day
I will come calling.

Growth

HE LAY THERE/LIFE REMEMBERED

A.A. Winston

He lay there
Lifeless.

Not as in life
Full of life
Life everlasting.

Giving life's energy
Through word
Deed
Thought.

Infusing life's blood
As he recollected
Looking back
Recounting stories
Reliving memories
Relishing people.

A life well lived
As he lay there.

UNFINISHED?

I cannot cry
For it is I
Who can see beyond
What lies ahead.

Growth

www.ingramcontent.com/pod-product-compliance
Lightning Source LLC
Chambersburg PA
CBHW021223130626
46554CB00004B/1341